To John [illegible]

In Season's Dream

For Lorraine,

John was a dear friend and I'd look forward to rotary each week because of his friendship - & how he loved the sea and had a great sense of humor!

I miss him each week, and was glad that he loved the walking stick I brought home from Ireland in 1985.

he was a tremendous presence.

Sincere regards,

Robert. Woburn May 2015

ISBN: Softcover 978-1-5035-5110-7
eBook 978-1-5035-5111-4

Print information available on the last page.

Rev. date: 03/11/2015

To order additional copies of this book, contact:
Xlibris
1-888-795-4274
www.Xlibris.com
Orders@Xlibris.com
708924

In Season's Dream

R. Tirrell Leonard Jr.

R. Tirrell Leonard Jr.

Edited by Tanya Gold

Contents

WINTER

John took a photo of me looking out the ballroom window once. The imagery I saw was used here.

Acknowledgements

I'd like to thank my wife Nancy. Thanks to Tanya Gold for her
Expertise in helping me shape this collection of poetry,
And all of my friends for countless stories and inspiration.

In July My friend Lee Richard White passed suddenly
I want to dedicate this volume to his memory.
I knew Lee only eight years, and since the first moment
He had referred to me as "The Dred Pirate" after one of his
Favorite movies… And sometimes just as "The Pirate."
Lee loved my first collection of poetry.
So I felt it fitting to dedicate this book to his daughter
Mollie White.

---R. Tirrell Leonard Jr.

Spring

On a Misty Spring Morn

I wander out in fog and rain
And listen to the pitter-pat.
I'm feeling wonder, as I strain
To wander out.

The veil of mists envelop fat
As fizzes forth a feeling vain,
It makes the buildings feel so flat.

My feelings by the sea constrain
On Derby Warf the sea froths splat,
And through the mists, a last domain—
To wander out.

I Hear Spring Coming

I hear spring coming through my window,
The birds and warm breath of air will stir
My thoughts and turn then, as if they know
I hear spring coming.

The soft sounds bring me to the sill and
Death to winter. I hear the crow call
The light of days and the soft shrill whir.

So soon, the green lush grasses shall grow
And give way to pleasant days, to blur
In passing hours as time sends us through.
I hear spring coming.

Songs of the Spirit

Songs in the silence, the hum of the rain,
Still in the evening, my muse, she will sing.
Surest of heart, so too feeling mundane
Songs in the silence, the hum of the rain,
Lulling and lively we wake her domain
Full of the sweetness, acute as a ping.
Songs in the silence, the hum of the rain,
Still in the evening, my muse, she will sing.

Tides

The tidewaters
Left the mud and stone
With shallow
Puddles of faith

Sinking in the mud
Drowning beneath the tides
Small puddles
Of faith

As the mud
Buried the bones
The question rose
"Where is God?"

Shallow puddles of faith
Never to see the light
Just going about their lives
While the tides
Kept rolling in

Nothing

I was dreaming of nothing this morn
As the birds were in song, for the light.
I was sleeping so near in a room,
On a couch by a window of the cape
As they rejoiced on branches of trees.
The shrill tunes had awoke me from sleep.
I lay there and enjoyed the shrill songs.
I was dreaming of nothing this morn.

Aloof, at Night

As the stars are all blinking at night
I watch the sky in delight
By the lake near a dark watermark.
The rings of Saturn are in sight.

The planets align and unite.
My thoughts are off-key, like a satellite.
In flight from the park is a meadow lark—
Undone, my dream, unwound from the night.

Thorns

For Juliet,
A pink rose—
Soft petals
Upon plumped lips.

Her blue eyes
Fixed open—
The organic
Velvet fabric.

Sadness
Lies beneath the skin,
As a wrinkle
In time's sheet.

Memories wrapped
In plastic lullabies,
Like melted wax
Sealing poison kisses.

Nature's Nymph

If were you, love, a flower
And were I but a field,
Your magic would delight me
In blossoms that ignite free.
I'd feel your tender power
Break through my raised shield.
If were you, love, a flower
And were I but a field.

If were you, love, the water
I'd drink from your tanned rune.
Spells to charm my existence
And sail across the distance.
For you are Love's own daughter
I sail by sun and moon.
If were you, love, the water
I'd drink from your tanned rune.

In your eyes, love, I could drown
And you would sing in mine.
By evening's sultry choral,
Your voice beneath the laurel
In your velvet, crimson gown.
So snares my heart's thin wine.
In your eyes, love, I could drown
And you would sing in mine.

If were you, love, a flower
And were I but a field,
Your magic would delight me
In blossoms that ignite free.
I'd feel your tender power
Break through my raised shield.
If were you, love, a flower
And were I but a field.

Chestnut Street

I take a walk down Chestnut Street—
Ancient of homes and beauty there.
I see a girl as soft as air.

She wanders shades of elms off-beat.
Sparrows singing so near to her
Affectionately twittering songs
To please her, woo her love for throngs
On branches jumping and flying.
And when the trees become alive
And colors change from green to red,
The birds all sing of winter's dread,
She listens still, to their sweet jive,
Soon and soft, the fall of snowflakes.
The sparrows sing of winter chills.
The girl with the rosy cheeks mills,
And waits for their swift songs. She aches.
And then the warmth of spring will come
As she dances beneath the trees,
The birds will all sing and fly like bees
Delighting her in streets, they'll thrum.

I saw a girl as soft as air.
Ancient of homes and beauty there.
I took a walk down Chestnut Street.

Summer

Refreshment on a Hot Day

In soaring, searing air—
I'm hiding from the heat.
Sweating humid despair
In soaring, searing air—
My thoughts are scrambled there.
A pools' edge cool retreat,
In soaring, searing air—
I'm hiding from the heat.

Sun Shower

Lilies are flowing with woven greens
As the rain is falling ever soft and yet cool,
A summer day hiding
Behind soft rolling gray clouds.

A crack thunders overhead
Yet, this shower is sunny
In almost Victorian gloom.
I stand and feel the rain,
My flesh, cool in pleasure.

A refreshing moment
In a rather hot day,
As sounds roil overhead
In thunderous glee.

Still, my lilies are flowing
Weaving color in the lush greens.

In a Suburban Meadow

My mind awakens sweetly, love
In the beauty of country fields,
In meadows, as butterflies dance
And float on wings of paper silk.

In coffee cups, my dreams renew
As spirits walk in summer songs
And stepping lush in greens and mint
A feeling cascades through my soul.

Fireflies in a Jar

I caught a bunch of fireflies
And sealed them in a glass jar.
Glowing green and blue of skies.
I caught a bunch of fireflies.
Behind glass, they long for skies,
Lights dimmed like a distant star.
I caught a bunch of fireflies
And sealed them in a glass jar.

The Common in Summer

(Washington Square, Salem Massachusetts)

Beneath the canopies of maple, beech and oak,
Oaken benches line the paths.
Paths of summer, lead to dreams of gold,
Golden lilies, butterflies and bees.
Bees simply buzz through the heated light—
Light filtering through the trees,
Trees to dream beneath.

Jetty's Edge

I walked towards the jetty's edge
And found my love up near the end,
She sat upon a granite stone
And watched the sea and moonbeams blend.

I walked towards the jetty's edge
To sit beside my love and watch
The waves reflect the stars of night,
On stonework seats up near the notch.

I walked towards the jetty's edge
And heard the waves upon the night.
The mists of sea splashed her and me.
We watched the sea, to much delight.

I walked towards the jetty's edge
And looked into the great unknown,
I held her hand so near the sea
As moonbeams reflected and atoned.

Windjammer

So far across a sun swept sea, a wind
Gently filled fabric sails with life
And left me dreaming on the beach.

As stars came to fill the sky
She rose above the campfire
Enticed me with a smile,

Caressed my worries with her
Gentle rhythms and lit my flesh
Aflame with supple grace, tenderly.

To yearn above this lustful wretch
And burning bright, within her embrace
As lost inside a smoldering fire.

So far across the sun-swept sea
She rose above my campfire—
Gentle rhythms ignited my flesh.

Burning bright within her touch,
Lost inside her desire,
Left to dream upon this beach,
Left to dream upon this beach.

Willow Moth

My younger days have filled my eyes.
Remember times beneath the boughs
Of tall and steady willow trees?

I saw a white fair butterfly
Flutter beneath a willow grove,
I called it my little willow moth.
I spied it often, there by willow row.

As I've grown to a stoutly man,
I noticed in my little willow moth
A gracefulness near my side.

One night beneath the moonlit row
As magic graced this willow grove,
I saw in my little willow moth
A metamorphosis of form and shape.

She seemed to grow in elfin grace
And there beneath the willow grove
I fell in love. For my little willow moth
Is beauty now inside my eyes and heart.

Another Bright Idea

Over and under
The boys flew all over,
They ran into hiding
As boys often did.
One tied a rope to his waist
Then lassoed a tree.
He swung over a breach
And went back and forth,
Not touching the ground.
Like a bird on a string.

Solitude

A clearing, just inside the woods
My slice of peace, on the small rug
Of grass that grew beneath
The canopy's lush green oval shape.

I'd lie for hours, staring skyward
As the light filtered through the trees,
Watching clouds drift across the space,
Morphing first into shapes, then dissolving.

When sounds of laughter would drift near
My brother and friends would pull me out
Of my reverie to play hide and seek
In the rusting white dry tall grass.

Or we'd dare to go inside the ruined
Foundation, where a fox would often live.
It's this space and its tuft of grass, I miss.
I often finding myself thinking about

Days when a boy's life could just be; to lie down
Staring into the sky on a tuft of grass, to dream.

Willow Breeze

The wind whispers through the willows,
Branching willows, gracing the isle.
Islands of time and northern thought,
Northern thinking, wafting in the breeze
Softly breeze by lit tallow tapers,
Tapering off my mind's clean edge.
Edging thoughts in soft willow glances,
Glancing through its cascading leaves,
Leaving much for me to contemplate.
Contemplation of time and space,
Spacing together the imagery of willows,
Willow trees, junipers, and wild finches.
Golden finches gracing fading lights of summer,
As summer gives way to paths of autumn.

Oblivion

Grey gleam of skies whose smile on wave and strand
Shines weary like a man's who smiles to know
That now no dream can mock his faith with show,
Nor cloud for him seem living sea or land.
--- From "A Solitude" by Algernon Charles Swinburne

I walk outside beneath the purple skies
As cooling breezes bring on thoughts of her,
And my flesh responds to the chills of night.
My senses calm as I watch the moon rise.
Night birds sing and rustle in nearby trees.
I'm captivated, strolling paths unplanned.
On moonlit paths I hear the ocean's song
And follow close to find the nearby shore,
But sounds obscure my view of starlit bands—
Grey gleam of skies whose smile on wave and strand.

The winds whip up the froth on crashing waves.
Soft pleasures, in chills, pass through my body
So like a dream inside this stream of air,
Like when we were walking on jetty rocks
When our hands touched and then the sounds howled.
We closed our eyes, and leaped across the show
As tendrils of desire had sparked our eyes.
What happened to us? Adrift since those days,
Watching starlight glinting off water that
Shines weary like a man's who smiles to know.

Remember watching the skies for cloud shapes?
Animals seen in puffs of steam or fog,
I kept you waiting far too long, I think,
Waiting as love passed like the phantom night.
What stills my heart, the simple pleasures near
The waning warmth of summer will winnow.
I feel my season changed and left behind,
Like days have ridden by me all at once
Tenderness lying beyond my grasp, though
That now no dream can mock his faith with show.

But when in bed, we read Swinburne's lines till dawn
And wondered of the course of human plight,
I knew my needs had lain within your love.
While toiling there to wrench into that life,
I lost my way and was adrift our hearts.
Standing on these cliffs the wind close at hand,
My thoughts of her cut and knives twist inside.
I see again, our hopes had dashed on rocks
And see no dreams to warm the hard wastelands
Nor cloud for him seem living sea or land.

Autumn

In Whispers

Soft winds
Ripple cool rains
And lines muddied
Beneath,
Dreaming,
The images
Dancing near oblivion
In rolling thunder.

In Quiet Moments

Silence seems to ring or buzz,
Eternally interrupted
By the sound of tires
On wet pavement.

The rain is falling coolly
Outside. The mist is sweeping nearer.
In such noise, I dream
Of pale moonlight

Just waiting to peak out
Behind purple clouds, in silence.

Beneath the Maple

I sit beneath
The orange glow
Of maple boughs
And stare off to dream.

The wind gently blows
The leaves to and fro,
Softly changing
From red, to orange and yellow.

I sit here to dream
By this mythic stream,
Beneath nature's reach
By this red maple tree.

So still, I continue sweeping,
These leaves seamlessly seeping.

Hurricane Sandy

On the winds are the sound's greedy howls
And the sea froths white on the caps.
I remember my faith in the land
As devils will take soon, with her growls
And her winds will ship fearsome commands.

We pray, for friends bracing her winds
As the storm blows through the old rough,
Till the moon will but shine, on the seas.
She will pass. And soon wither her winds
In the width of her strength, full enough.

Vapors

Twisted up and out
Of earthen pines,
The organic faceless phantom
Dances, twists
In the cool night winds.

Is it a creature
Of some hellish whim,
Or merely
A shallow puddle
Of murky faith?

As the pale moonlight
Shows gently down,
It seems to wither
And further decay,

Rapidly transforms
Into dustlings
Blown upon
These eastern winds.

In Falling Leaves

Air crisp and leaves crunch beneath my step,
It smells of fall, on winds, in rustling leaves.
The days are cooler, crisper breezes prep
Air crisp and leaves crunch beneath my step
As whispered words of haunting songs in step.
Such homes and feelings, dance beneath the eaves
Air crisp and leaves crunch beneath my step
It smells of fall, on winds, in rustling leaves.

The Locomotive God

Searching for the Locomotive God
Under the rush of falling dominoes,
I reach up, as if for stars,
And land in muddy puddles.

Pumpkins grin along the path.

The patch by the orchard's grove lies serene
But the squashes seem obscene.
Walking on the autumnal road,
I feel the Northerly winds, whipping falling leaves.

I cherish the scents of clove in chimney smoke.

A smile plays upon my lips, as I watch
A spider gently spin her web.
Backlit by star and moonlight,
She waits, for a meal soon trapped.

Her web glints in silvery pale light.

And just beyond the tree line, there once stood
A rusting engine on forgotten tracks,
A fading relic, rusted into the northern wood.
I feel a sadness here, of life left behind.

In ghostly steam, there a century stood.

At Storm's End

Up at night, I saw the clouds and moon
And I traced the thin lines out across
My thoughts and my prayers, to the last rune.
Up at night, I saw the clouds and moon
On the winds as the whispers attuned
To my sense of the songs of great loss.
Up at night, I saw the clouds and moon
And I traced the thin lines out across
To the lights all in flickers that swoon.
Up at night, I saw the clouds and moon
So I watched, on my stoop as too soon
The glow in the clouds embossed.
Up at night, I saw the clouds and moon
And I traced the thin lines out across.

Fate

The leaves falling, cascading around my form,
A form of twirling winds, of autumn hush,
A hushing feel of watching birds at play.
Playing children are filling dreams of lore.

A darker lore of deathly hallowed storm,
A storm that bellows decades flowing blush,
In which blushing maids fill their earthly clay,
A reddish clay, of milk and honeyed war.

The war of darker meanings here informs,
Informing times to wake the days so lush,
So luscious news of ripened flesh today.
Today is bound as God's own palm, adores

Adoring souls who seek a fallen norm,
The norms no longer pliable, but flush.

The Stations

So softly, graces flow like a sweet breeze
Reminding me I love to walk outside.
Autumn mornings I find a lovely guide
To walk beneath the bowers here with ease.

The pond's a pretty walk, light is our stride.
As color brightly changes tree and shrub,
My thoughts of you, dear Lord, a warmer hub
And her, my companion, my lovely bride.

But when I feel the swell alone to scrub
Emotions, a tidal surge beckons me kneel.
Before I'm faced with God, I ask to feel.
This night shall pass one day, so true a snub.

Sunshine will warm my face and soul to heal,
In wounds, He cleans my sins. In grace, surreal.

Numbered Are the Hours

I walk the reach, a long paved path
Between the swamp and pond
And hear the calls of geese and ducks
Beyond the veils of fog.
As if my time were calling forth
I see the isle near,
Her willows eerie in the mist.
As thoughts so stamped in Stoker's words,
Despair has its own calms.
My pulse quickens, and so the dream of life,
As I know, yet Charon waits patiently
And one day, I'll ride his ancient boat
To float beyond the veil,
And touch the isle's beach out there
Where none has ever returned.

Winter

Endurance

The cold was seeping
Deep within
As winds and rain
Froze my soul.
A whisper from my
Lips arose
Unheard and carried
By the winds.

Once Past

It was a life I dreamed of living long ago.
So now I watch the winter frost the glass,
And winds of ice will chill my memory, although
To me, it sings of her somewhere in past.
In shades of love, these spans of trees had cried their leaves.
It was a life, I dreamed of living long ago.

In Natural Beauty

A theme of pain is wound inside my mind.
What dream is there, to soften changes blind?

I watch the snow in falling sheets and feel
The loss of time, as moods shift all around
From fall leaves to this first soft snow, I kneel.

I dance in Nature's arms, in her long dress.
Beneath the boughs of winter trees, we kiss.
On through the fields a choral tune will hiss
As once beneath the arbors of wild oak trees.

In boats beneath the moon, we ride the keel
And swells bring forth from us a song unbound,
To sail on tides of evermore and reel.

What dream is there, to soften changes blind?
A theme of pain is wound inside my mind.

A Christmas Wreath

I wander down the wooded path,
Paths lined in junipers, firs and pines.
Pine-scented cones in the blissful chill,
Chilling my bones beneath the falling flakes.
Snowflakes glistening beneath the moonlit glow,
Glowing upon the echoes of my heart and home.
As scents of home drift in my mind
Minding the coming winter weather.
As weathering another time or place,
Placing Christmas so near, as my soul will trace
Will trace the lines of the falling flakes.

Ison

And so I breathe in through this mask
As if my cold were all but done,
The racking cough that woke my slumber
Put to dust as Christmas lumber.

Feeling like a flue taking root,
I dream on stars so far and wide,
A cosmic realm beyond my sight
While my breath takes on this blight.

It speeds on to our cosmic shores
With fiery plumes of steam dispelled,
A notion of Ison, herald of the night
Will leave my sleep in fits, of mortal flight.

Trapped In Fields of Ice

I had heard they got trapped in the fields of the ice,
Pleasure cruise and ice breaker waited in the cold.
They dreamed of a thaw and the melting of ice
Yet were there, in the cold of the southern seas hold.

While the news that had then broke on radio that day,
The Xue Long, the ice breaker, was stuck in the fields
And the sea's ice was double as thick, in a way.
Ah, so much for a theory of melting, who yields?

For the winds of the world are now cooling out here,
You can feel it in chills, as if fate has begun.
In the drop of some dice, or the snows howling there
Yet, the needle still drops as the ghosts are but done.

In the heat from the sun, does the earth slowly cool
Or will winter endure, and still make us a fool?

In His Cups

The empty words are sounding hollow now
As drops of golden whiskey dregs avow.

The coldest winter gives the mind excuse
To crave for more and dream inside the glass,
As licking final drops on shards of blues.

Sunlight filters inside a dirty pane
Refracting through the empty bottles near,
To wake a soul, so far away from cheer
So bleary eyes will squint and feel as slain.

In glasses, pictures stain the mind and show
A feeling lost along the way's bypass,
To leave in snail or bottle shell tattoos.

As drops of golden whiskey dregs avow
The empty words are sounding hollow now.

In the Veil

On the winds, falling snow so adrift
As it fell in a veil and a mist.
So I paused as it fell and still fell,
As my foot had a print as I walked.
So I thought of the moon and the squall,
As a dream, as I walked in the veil.

In my sleep, snow misted as it fell,
And the waves of the storm and the winds...
I awoke from the dream of the squall,
With the wolves of the mist still unseen,
On a walk in the veil of the night
Full of songs of the winds and the snow.

A soft pulse is now felt in my dreams
Of the winds and the veils of soft snow.

Of Moonlit Dreams

Still listening to Beethoven, one can believe
In woven dreams, of what magic was once called love.
As clouds so move in winter skies, I hear his songs.
A sonata so sown of sweet enchantments still

So what, do tell me now, of what is love today?
I see but war and hatred curse a world, so vexed
I once had seen a dream, I knew, was love a dream?
Or was it fate? Oh, she of light and roses sweet.

I watch the seas, as moonlight splashes winter light
Recalling dreams, immortal tones of music here;
I can believe in dreams of her, while worlds are moved
In grace and light, she sings of sweetest beauty still.

Recalling here a dream's enchantment, once called love
As tidal crushes sand and shore, a dream yet lives.

Sketch In Blank Verse

I

Relics of houses, standing stout, attest
To moral fibers lost. A vague outline
In disrepair, its shingles, failing walls
Are creaking, needing care. Still, breathing haunts
A grimly silhouette half-dead in time,
It may reduce to ash, but here it stands.
It stands as things do, slaking grim solace
To grind a stone to dust and rise again.
Relics of houses, standing stout, attest.

II

The winter snow has blanketed the lands
It covers woods; the garden world is iced.
Still birds are singing, fawns are prancing
Rays of sunshine warming the signs of life.
While deer and elk sip of streams in this calm,
The garden has reclaimed the lands of men
Adam nor Eve are sensed, as they are dreams;
The winter snow has blanketed the lands.

III

The shadows seen here, on woodland edges
A moment here or there, now ghosts of grand
Violent and graceful pasts, silent remnants
Of men. The speed of fate, unnoticed, slips
By, and in fear arise the loud protests
While death claims this world of men and shudders
When fiery rockets fall from the skies
On cities burning, men alone will run—
A flight to hills of darker woods to breathe
As shadows seen here, on woodland edges.

Thoughts in Curls of Snow

So still and silent in the winter winds,
So like the ice-encrusted maple trees,
I feel alone. The world of light rescinds.

The darker hints of threads in mythic hymns,
I stand at best, in still and stormy breeze,
So still and silent in the winter winds.

A vibrant chord, rings my bells by the winds
And swells inside my heart, a mere disease.
I feel alone. The world of light rescinds.

Yet life degrades my soul of light, it dims
My heart in vexing, waxing, sound degrees,
So still and silent in the winter winds.

Has love abandoned me? Outside the winds
Of time are seen in shades of darker keys.
I feel alone. The world of light rescinds.

The snow curls beneath the light of my sins
In weights of faith. I feel the pulls and freeze,
So still and silent in the winter winds,
I feel alone. The world of light rescinds.

In Thin Steam

My winter months are longing.
In dreams the cold will sing.
Now birds sing near on branches,
Sad as the world now blanches.
I wait in snow, prolonging
As songs, sweetly trilling,
My winter months are longing.
In dreams the cold will sing.

While I sit beside the fire
And warm my bones, I dream
And think of her sweet beauty
A long lost willing duty.
Now my soul is lit afire
In phantoms of thin steam.
While I sit beside the fire
And warm my bones, I dream.

My winter months are longing.
In dreams the cold will sing.
Now birds sing near on branches,
Sad as the world now blanches.
I wait in snow, prolonging
As songs, sweetly trilling,
My winter months are longing.
In dreams the cold will sing.

A Wish Out On the Stars

A walk beneath the tree lines
While the birds sang sweetly
Could send my heart abounding
To stars all lit and rounding.
So I stop here as she shines,
Feeling blue completely—
A walk beneath the tree lines
While the birds sang sweetly.

A mere thanks wouldn't do here
As I light the candle.
My faith is dark and brooding,
My heart is now deluding
In part, I see a clue near
For my heart's a vandal—
A mere thanks wouldn't do here
As I light the candle.

So here, beneath the moonlight,
I begin to wonder,
Cross-seas the shore is distant
The wake of hearts resistant
It feels like a monsoon's night
Like soul's rent asunder—
So here, beneath the moonlight,
I begin to wonder.

As the hours near to Christmas
See the world in winter,
The hearts of giving kindness
Forgive the sons of blindness.
'Neath the stars an unkissed lass
Shines brighter midwinter—
As the hours near to Christmas
See the world in winter.

The Snow Queen

As snow falls down
On past, the window panes,
The parks white gown
Spreads through the idle lanes.
Out in the snow,
My mind will stroll beneath
In the days glow.
Chills will dance underneath.
Beneath crystals
Of frozen Oakwood trees,
Lay iced pistils
Of lilies left to freeze.
And as the sun
Sets upon this scene,
The time does run
To daylight's dancing queen.
An elfin girl
In winter's charming robes,
Of frost and twirl.
My heart's struck by her probes
And by the streams
Beneath the frozen moon.
I dance in beams
And listen to the loon.
She holds the key
Of our love's tender chains
And locks a plea,
Of phantoms icy reigns.

The Elemental

In the dark, the oil-lantern illuminated path
Down spiral stone cut stairs,
Crept farther into dampened earth.

The organic smells of soil, mold, dust and rot
Lingered in the musty air. I felt nervous.
As dripping sounds echoed in the walls, I listened.

Clearing cobwebs from an ancient doorway
I tried not to think of what abandoned those webs
Of feathery dust gowns. The shadows played on my nerves.

Still I heard the echoing sounds of dripping water.
As I drew nearer, I saw a glow
Flickering and cascading across the stones.

When I rounded a corner, I found myself
Within a chamber lit
By a campfire, tended by a sitting figure.

His graying hair and deep wrinkled flesh
Surrounded deep-set knowing blue eyes.
He sat on a bench, prodding the flames.
He was dressed in pale blue linen garments
Beneath a dark brownish cloak,
To me, he cut a weird and strange figure.

His garments seemed to flow above
His left shoulder and gather by his torso,
Draping to his knees, like a kilt.

His shoes were more like leather sandals
And cracked from years of wear,
Sparks rose from the fire as he prodded

Clearing his throat, he finally spoke.
"I've been waiting for you," he said.
I noticed then, beyond him, a wall of ice.

"What are you?" I asked, "what is that shape
Inside the ice?" a huge dark creature was
Trapped inside the ice, from end to end.

He calmly spoke to me then, "I'm a watcher
And I am getting old, for when I leave
The ice will wreath the world in eternal winter."

"You," he said, pointing the charred end of his stick
In my general direction, "Have been called
To replace me, in this place."

"But," I said, panic in my eyes and voice,
"I am only a human, a mortal that will someday die
What is there that I could do?"

He tossed his stick into the fire, stood and yawned,
Stretching widely, as I heard the crackling of his bones.
And he stared as if for centuries, into my eyes.

He began to fade into vapors, his eyes staring into mine.
His voice I heard as if from inside my head,
"Then the demon shall be released from his bondage."

He was gone from the room and I sat by the fire.
I began to tend it as my own, feeling its warmth.
I heard a faint voice, anguished, "You are the watcher.
This world will end, frozen in winter's white."

Fragment

The tin roof of the quaint wooden structure
Brimmed with snow, falling down on the hill.
A tall man with slumped shoulders looked over
The small ranch, sunlight glinting off the roof.
It spoke of poverty and the tall man
Felt the strength passing through his veins and sighed.
Silently, snow falling from the sky, no birds
In flight or song, no howling winds to sweep,
Just quiet. He leaned on his shovel
And watched the scene a moment more, to think.

He walked quickly towards his modest home
In the sullen mood of a snowy day.
He was seeking warmth, as he thought of her.
And in turning back to the filling woods
He searched his mind for her, as it snowed on.
Church bells rang off far in town and brought him
Back to days when they were young and in love.

He'd bring her flowers nearly every day,
He'd brought them in the hospital that day.
The echo of her laugh rang in his ears.
He wiped his eyes at memories of her mirth
and felt his age set in his bones.

He put a kettle on for some tea.
She'd been gone ten years now. When he forgot
Her withering in that bed, pain racking
As she coughed and had little appetite,
The doctors talking of cancer and treatments...
He was a wreck. And now he was alone.

When he thought of her voice as musical
Or mistook her for a shadow from a
Corner of his eye, she danced as a ghost.

She had gone quietly as the snow fell.
He had placed yellow daffodils, her favorite,
In a white vase before her.
She smiled as the light began her fading
"You'll keep these at home for me, now won't you?"

Like some winter dreams, as the kettle steamed
He poured his tea and sipped, thinking of her.
The white vase sat still, with the dried flowers.
"So God, I must ask you what you think of
Humanities quest to live forever?"
He huffed in his rusty deep voice and sighed.
"I forget, you keep quiet with your cards."
His questions circled in his mind and thoughts.
He'd rather think of her than question God.
He never helped them as she slipped away.
And still he looked at the dried daffodils
He thought to get on a whim that day.

He stood with his tea and, sipping, went near
The window and watched the world of winter,
His statements unnoticed by the dust.
He thought of how delighted she was
To see those yellow flowers in the vase.
Maybe God did help, in some tiny way.

He watched the flakes coming down again
And wondered if she was waiting for him, or if
The vale held no comforts in the cold dark.
Her laughter was the very thing he missed.
He peered out into nothing, lost in thought.

Often he measured time by weight of snow.

Other Books by R. Tirrell Leonard Jr

Poetry

In The Murmuring Trees, 2012

Praise for In The Murmuring Trees

"Imaginative poems and prose of great spirit, rich creativity, and three-dimensional imagery." The Columbia Review.

“Drawing inspiration from sources as diverse as Robert Frost, Charles Dickens, William Faulkner, Edgar Allen Poe, and the New England Transcendentalists, R. Tirrell Leonard Jr.'s poetry collection, *In The Murmuring Trees*, combines an admirable ambition of poetic style with a deep sympathy and appreciation for the fields, rivers and woodlands of his native Massachusetts.” The Blue Ink Review

The poems in this book explore the delicate balance between man & nature, the impulse to see figures for our emotions everywhere around us, & the way the world can speak our own thoughts & feelings back to us so eloquently.

The book isn't broken into sections of any type & this seems like a problem since the book is so unrelenting in its messages, never giving the reader a chance to pause & process, a necessary break to digest all of what is happening.

A poem like "Thistle Rush" demonstrates what's most heartily at work in this collection. The couplet stanza pattern really paces out the beauty here, & while the poem is one of physical love, we're given a glimpse of the spiritual.

--Judge, Writer's Digest 21st Annual Self-Published Book Awards

"A fine knack for writing poetry"--- Jordan Rich, WBZ/CBS News Radio Boston, The Jordan Rich Show

Citations

Poems previously published on the web

Oblivion had previously appeared on the web : http://www.writersdigest.com/forum/viewtopic.php?f=34&p=512971

Oblivion, Sat April 20, 2013 8:20am

I wrote Oblivion for The Poem a Day challenge of Writer's Digest's Robert Lee Brewer's Poetic asides.

ROBERT J. LEONARD
176 MONTVALE AVE
WOBURN, MA 01801

CPSIA information can be obtained at www.ICGtesting.com
Printed in the USA
LVOW10s1802190415
435221LV00001B/154/P